MANNERS AT SCHOOL

by Emma Bassier

Cody Koala

An Imprint of Pop!

popbooksonline.com

abdobooks.com
Published by Pop!, a division of ABDO, PO Box 398166, Minneapolis, Minnesota 55439.

Printed in the United States of America, North Mankato, Minnesota

102019
012020

THIS BOOK CONTAINS RECYCLED MATERIALS

Cover Photo: iStockphoto
Interior Photos: iStockphoto, 1, 5, 6, 7, 8, 11, 13, 15, 16–17, 19 (bottom left), 19 (bottom right), 21 (top left), 21 (top right), 21 (bottom); Shutterstock Images, 19 (top)

Editor: Brienna Rossiter
Series Designer: Jake Slavik

Library of Congress Control Number: 2019942419

Publisher's Cataloging-in-Publication Data
Names: Bassier, Emma, author.
Title: Manners at school / by Emma Bassier
Description: Minneapolis, Minnesota : Pop!, 2020 | Series: Manners matter | Includes online resources and index.
Identifiers: ISBN 9781532165610 (lib. bdg.) | ISBN 9781644942949 (pbk.) | ISBN 9781532166938 (ebook)
Subjects: LCSH: Manners--Juvenile literature. | Polite behavior--Juvenile literature. | Schools--Juvenile literature. | Social customs--Juvenile literature. | Classroom environment--Juvenile literature.
Classification: DDC 395.12--dc23

Hello! My name is

Cody Koala

Pop open this book and you'll find QR codes like this one, loaded with information, so you can learn even more!

Scan this code* and others like it while you read, or visit the website below to make this book pop.

popbooksonline.com/manners-at-school

*Scanning QR codes requires a web-enabled smart device with a QR code reader app and a camera.

Table of Contents

Chapter 1

Time to Learn

A bell rings. School starts. Students sit at desks. They stay quiet as the teacher talks. They are using good manners.

Watch a video here!

Manners are the correct words or actions for certain situations. A school has many people and many rooms.

In each place, students show manners in different ways.

Raising a hand is a **polite** way to get the teacher's attention.

Students work together to take care of their classroom. They clean up messes. They are gentle with books and supplies. And they put things back after using them.

Chapter 2

In the Classroom

During class, students should show **respect** for others. Listen when someone else is talking. Don't **interrupt** or make loud noises.

Learn more here!

Remember to use kind words. Don't **gossip** or **tattle**. Instead, think of others before you speak. Imagine how you would feel if someone said the same thing about you.

Saying *please* and *thank you* shows good manners too.

Chapter 3

In the Halls

It is **polite** to line up right away when the teacher asks. Once you're in line, stand quietly. Don't push or cut in line.

Complete an activity here!

In the hallways, stay with the rest of the class. Always walk instead of running. Also, keep your voice soft.

Students in other classes are learning. By staying quiet, you will not **distract** them.

Chapter 4

Other Places

Students eat lunch in the cafeteria. To be **polite**, stay seated while eating. Don't talk with your mouth full. And remember to clean up your trash.

Learn more here!

Students use manners at **recess** too. They may go to a playground or gym. They share toys and take turns. By thinking of others, students help everyone have fun.

Raise your hand.

Keep voices quiet.

Help keep the classroom clean.

Making Connections

Text-to-Self

Students go to school to learn. What is your favorite topic to learn about?

Text-to-Text

Have you read other books about manners? How were those manners similar to or different from the manners described in this book?

Text-to-World

People use manners when they are in school. Where else can you use manners?

Glossary

distract – to take someone's attention away from what he or she is trying to focus on.

gossip – to say unkind words about other people without them knowing.

interrupt – to start talking while someone else is still talking.

polite – showing good manners.

respect – a way of treating others that shows you care about their thoughts and feelings.

tattle – to tell what someone else is doing wrong in order to get him or her in trouble.

Index

Online Resources

popbooksonline.com

Thanks for reading this Cody Koala book!

Scan this code* and others like it in this book, or visit the website below to make this book pop!

popbooksonline.com/manners-at-school

*Scanning QR codes requires a web-enabled smart device with a QR code reader app and a camera.